GREENS

Poems by Arnold Adoff

Illustrated by Betsy Lewin

Lothrop, Lee & Shepard Books   New York

Text copyright © 1988 by Arnold Adoff
Illustrations copyright © 1988 by Betsy Lewin
All rights reserved. No part of this book may be reproduced or utilized in any form or by any means, electronic or mechanical, including photocopying, recording or by any information storage and retrieval system, without permission in writing from the Publisher. Inquiries should be addressed to Lothrop, Lee & Shepard Books, a division of William Morrow & Company, Inc., 105 Madison Avenue, New York, New York 10016. Printed in the United States of America.

First Edition 1 2 3 4 5 6 7 8 9 10

Library of Congress Cataloging in Publication Data
Adoff, Arnold. Greens.
Summary: Illustrated poems about the color green. 1. Green — Juvenile poetry. 2. Children's poetry, American. [1. Green — Poetry. 2. American poetry] I. Lewin, Betsy, ill. II. Title. PS3551.D66G7 1987 811'.54
85-16631
ISBN 0-688-04276-7   ISBN 0-688-04277-5 (lib. bdg.)

Mobile

For
Ker
Mit
The
    Frog
    With
    This
    Kiss
And
Hug
For
    Being
    Green
And
For
His
    Green Song

    Live Long

Green kite in March breeze
　　　　　　　Diving
　　　　Into
　　　　　　March　trees
Just
Beginning to
　　　　　　Bud
Green

Hold tight
　　　　And this
　　　　　　Thin white
　　　　　　　　String
Will
Pull you into the
　　　　　　Next　season
Will
Pull you into
　　　　　　A
Green Spring

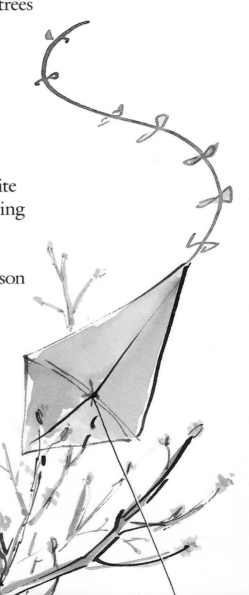
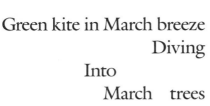

In The Heavy Spring Breeze

The green leaves   the hundreds
                              Of
      Green leaves
                  Each a different shade
Flash
      And
Turn
Like hundreds of green tops
                  Spinning
Like hundreds of green tops
                  Along the top of the cottonwood tree

They are greeting the new season
                        Spinning into Spring
            Greeting me
Just
Made for me

9

Caterpillar to the leaf
Leaf to the stem of the leaf
Stem of the leaf
To the twig
Twig

To the branch
Branch

To the trunk
Trunk

Trunk of the tree
In
To the
Green
Ground
Of
Spring

As Soon As She Is Up

Grandma is up
          And
          Out   side
Picking the
Fresh
          And
            New
          And
          Tender

          Dandelion greens   to
                         Cook
                         Up
                         For
                         Us
                         All

All Day Long

Green
Grass hoppers hop
                  High
Fly by
      My
Feet   in the high grass

Instant replay
              And
          Repeat

Green
Grass hoppers hop
                  High

Fly by
My
Feet   in the high grass
And
Repeat

All day long
Song

Grass

Green and
Greener
    Than
Green
    A
Thousand
Shades in the noon
      Day
      Sun
      Un
      Der
My running feet

14

O
Grass
  O
Grass
   O
Green
Grass
    Wr$_{in}$kl$_{in}$
       g
Under my feet

    I know the next
       Shower
    Will
S t r a i g h t e n you out

    I want to grow
     That
    S
    t
    r
    a
    i
    g
    h
    t
     That
     Fast

15

Under the hottest Summer sun
Green garden hose
Is
My shower
Fills
My pool
Keeps
Me cool
And
Waters the dusty flowers   I planted in the
Spring

Green garden hose
Is the best thing
Under the hottest Summer sun
Is
The
Most fun

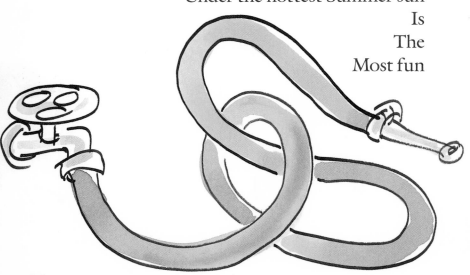

Summer Leaves

        Are
        At their brightest
            Green
On the bushes
        Outside my window
        But
It
Is the
  Red berries that bring
    The hungry birds

Momma Drives

       This
       Pick
        Up
Truck
    Full of
Newspapers
        To
The
   Re
   Cycle
   Center   and I help carry
           The bags inside

Momma drives and I am along
               To work
And
For the good talk
  This good ride

Green Truck

      Stuck
In brown
      Mud

      Tan
     Woman
With
     Red face
Kicks
   Gray
      Stone
Kicks
   Green
      Truck

We walk
   Back
To our
     Place
Talking
    About
   Bad luck

In The Fall After The First Frost

All
The trees will turn
Their Autumn shades of
                        Tan
                        And
                        Red
And gold and brown

                    Yellow

But green hides
            Under
    Snow
                Until
Spring

The
Old
Tin
    Roof
      Of
The
    House   is a bright green thing
               Showing
                        The promise of
                                Next
                                Spring

Through the
              Snowing
Afternoon

21

Ever
Greens

      Are
Darkest
Green are
Almost
Black
Against   the
      White snow
          And
          The bright blue sky
               Shows
          Cold and still
          In the winter after
               Noon

We stay
    Back
We play   inside by the fire

In My Coloring Book

This green van
With
This green man
From   far
Beyond   Mars
From
Beyond   our
Stars   is   driving   down
My PaperAndCrayons
Street

He
Says he wants to meet my mother
But
She is looking the other way
And
He cannot stay
For the next
Page

23

One night   Kermit The Frog was riding along
On the back
Of the Loch
     Ness Monster
Through
     The waters of the Hudson
        River

On their way out to sea
     To the
Atlantic Ocean
And back to Scotland
     Kermit was singing his   special
        Song
     And the Loch Ness Monster Was
        Wag
          g
          i
          n
          g

His great
     Green tail along   just right

I know they were happy in the night

From the dark
         Green
        Atlantic
      Deep
One
    Flashing
       Blue
And white
       Fin
One
    Swordfish
      Fin
       Cutting

    The green water
      Like
A moving knife

    Leaping
     In

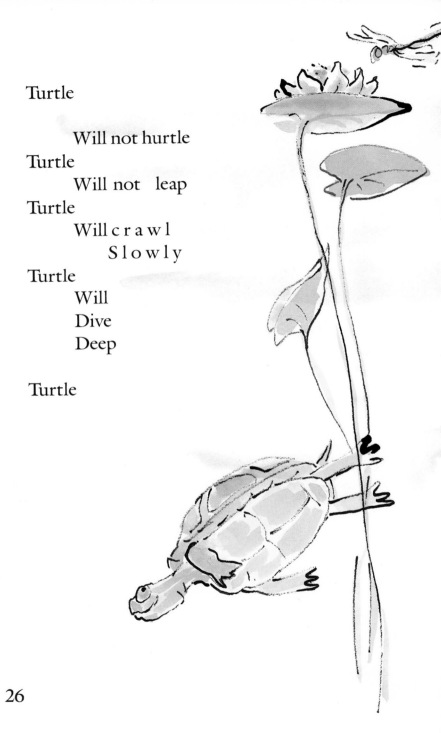

Turtle

      Will not hurtle
Turtle
      Will not   leap
Turtle
      Will c r a w l
            S l o w l y
Turtle
      Will
      Dive
      Deep

Turtle

I am tired of coloring green
                              Grass
                              Green
And red
            Apples
        Red
        And faces pink and brown

        Yellow hair on a
                    Tan   round
                              Head
        Or another red nose on a
                              White
                              Face
                              Clown

I want a red lawn instead of green
And an orange banana a purple frog
                        On a purple log
                              And
A tasty black green bean

I want a green woman and a green man
With all our faces colored the same
                        In this green
                              Game

A Green Monster Face

Is staring from the
                    M i d d l e
Of my split pea soup
Is
Not
        Scaring me with
                        His
        Split pea eye
                        His
        Split pea grin

I dip my spoon right
                    In
And race him   to
                    The
            B o t t o m
Of the bowl

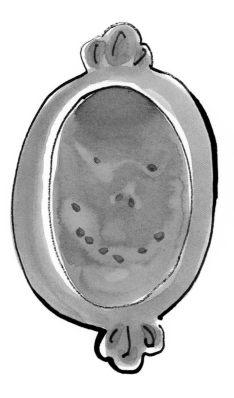

He disappears without a trace
                            And
The split pea grin
                Is on my face

28

Greens to the left
                    Of
                    Me
Greens to the
                    Right
Greens are climbing
                    Up
                    My
                    Fork
                    So
Momma
          Now I bite

Beans
      To the north
             Of
             Me
Beans
      To the   south

Beans
      Are
Leaning   on my chin
      Are
Sliding   in my
          Mouth

GREEN SKIRT
GREEN HAT

GREEN SHIRT
THE
SAME

WITH

ORANGE
LETTERS

THAT
PROCLAIM

NOTRE DAME

31

At Christmas Time I Open My Banks

And pile my nickles
        Quarters
         Dimes   to spend for
                     Presents
                         And
                    There is
                    Always a
                    Little extra
                    To lend my
                         Sister
                       Interest
                         Free

For me
A low hill of wrinkled dollar bills
That will buy my dad this shirt
                           That
        Will buy my mom this green
                       Plant

At Christmas time   I open my banks
And change my money into thanks

Greta

This
Baby 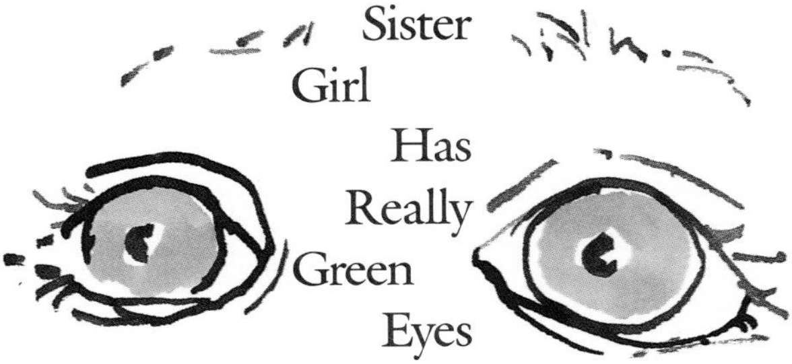
Sister
Girl
Has
Really
Green
Eyes
That
Shine
Into
Mine

Such
Fine
Eyes
Such
Fine
Family
Eyes

Greens

Pistachio ice cream   grass   trees   leaves   Jell-O
          My best green jacket lying in the snow
                    And   smelly   cheese

Lettuce
Cabbage   all the parts of a grasshopper
                    Standing very still
          The green
                    Blur   of a grasshopper
                              Hopp
                                   ing
          Down my best green hill
                    And green peas

Beautiful broccoli   awful sour apples   a sweet plum
                         And under this thumb
My green pen writing green
                    Words that please and rhyme
                    And mean I am doing my best

All the rest   is other colors   for   another   time

Arnold Adoff

believes that "writing a poem is making music with words and space," and that *Greens* is "a young book, full of music and rhythm and *much rhyme*." He was born and educated in New York City and has been writing "some kind of poetry" since adolescence. Now a noted author, poet, and anthologist, he has published fifteen books of poetry, including ALA Notables *Eats* and *All the Colors of the Race,* for Lothrop. Mr. Adoff and his wife, the author Virginia Hamilton, are Distinguished Visiting Professors at Queens College in New York City.

Betsy Lewin's

charming illustrations have appeared in *Furlie Cat* by Berniece Freschet and *Penny* by Beatrice Schenk de Regniers. The artist lives in Brooklyn, New York.